Kamisama Kiss

D1224447

19

Story & Art by

Julietta Suzuki

Kamisama Kiss

Volume 19
CONTENTS

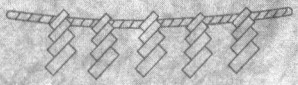

Chapter 108 004
Chapter 109 037
Chapter 110 067
Chapter 111 097
Chapter 112 129
Chapter 113 162
End Notes 196

CHARACTERS

Tomoe

The shinshi who serves Nanami now that she's a tochigami. Originally a wild fox ayakashi. He controls powerful kitsunebi.

Nanami Momozono

A high school student who was turned into a kamisama by the tochigami Mikage. She likes Tomoe.

Onikiri

Onibi-warashi, spirits of the shrine.

Kotetsu

Onibi-warashi, spirits of the shrine.

Mamoru

Nanami's shikigami. He can create a spiritual barrier to keep out evil.

Kurama

A super-popular idol. He's actually a tengu.

Mizuki

Nanami's second shinshi. The incarnation of a white snake. Used to be the shinshi of Yonomori shrine.

Unari

The chief of the mermaids who rule over the Okinawan sea. Kirihito stole her robe of feathers.

Kirihito

A human whose body was taken over by the great yokai Akura-oh. He is attended by shikigami minions.

Story so far

Nanami Momozono is a high school student who was evicted from her home when her dad skipped town.
She meets the tochigami Mikage at a park, and he leaves his shrine and his kami powers to her.
Now Nanami spends her days with Tomoe and Mizuki, her shinshi, and with Onikiri and Kotetsu, the onibi-warashi spirits of the shrine.
Nanami has been slowly gaining powers as kamisama by holding a festival at her shrine, attending a big kami conference, and all sorts of other adventures.
Nanami's and Tomoe's feelings for each other are finally out in the open and they have started to date!
Nanami and her classmates go on a school trip to Okinawa. The mermaid Unari suspects Ami of stealing her robe of feathers and kidnaps her. Kikuichi, Kirihito's minion, bargains with Nanami to help Kirihito in exchange for the robe, and then...

Kamisama Kiss
Chapter 108

WHAT ARE A YOKAI AND A HUMAN DOING HERE?
THIS ISN'T GOOD!
I DID NOT WANT...
LONG TIME NO SEE, FOX JERK.
...THE FOX AND KIRIHITO-DONO...
...RUNNING INTO EACH OTHER.
FWOOSH

WHACK
WHA?
YOU'RE THE YOKAI WHO WAS SCURRYING AROUND MOUNT KURAMA.
DID YOU CAUSE THIS MESS TOO?
GOOD!
I'LL TAKE KIRIHITO-SAMA—
WHAT'RE YOU SCHEMING?

HEY, FOX! WAIT!
OW OW!
KIRI-HITO-DONO!
I RECOG-NIZE THAT KNIFE.
STAB
HE'S THE BRAT I SAW IN THE LAND OF THE DEAD.
I KNOW YOU'VE COME HERE...
...TO LOOK FOR YOUR MASTER, LIKE A PATHETIC PUPPY.

SHE'S QUIET NOW BECAUSE I SUCKED HER LIFE ENERGY DRY.
SHE KEPT WAILING AND CALLING YOUR NAME.
SHE ALREADY FED ME.
TOO BAD YOU DIDN'T MAKE IT IN TIME.
K-KIRI-HITO-SAMA!
SO, IDIOT FOX. HOW DO YOU FEEL ABOUT YOUR MASTER BEING HALF DEAD?
A HUMAN KAMI IS SO CONVENIENT.
BUT I'VE COM-PLETELY RECOV-ERED.
BAS-TARD!
CRUNCH
YOU NEVER ARRIVE ON TIME, DO YOU?

KILL ME IF YOU CAN!
HOW DARE YOU TALK TO ME THAT WAY!
YOU WORM! I'LL KILL YOU!
FWOOSH
DIE!
KIRIHITO-SAMA!

FLASH
KIKU-ICHI!
...
YOU'RE NOT WELL ENOUGH TO FIGHT THAT FOX.
NO, KIRIHITO-SAMA...
DON'T BUTT IN!
I WON'T LET YOU RUN AWAY!
I WILL.
YOU TAKE CARE OF THE FOX, KIKUICHI-DONO. ♡
YATORI-DONO! TAKE KIRIHITO-SAMA AWAY!

THUD
THAT ARM...
...IS MY TOKEN OF GRATITUDE.
THE HUMAN KAMI IS SLEEPING IN THE HUT OVER THERE.
GO RESCUE HER. SHE'S VERY FRAIL...
NANAMI!
FWF
NANAMI!
DAMMIT!

POKE
POKE
Pop

I HEARD TOMOE'S VOICE FROM FAR AWAY.
HE'S VERY ANGRY...
HE'LL YELL AT ME...
YOU FOOL. YOU STICK YOUR NOSE INTO ANYTHING, BUT YOU'RE WEAK LIKE A WORM.
LIKE THIS...
TOMOE ...
...IS THOUGHTFUL AND RELIABLE ...
HE'S NOT LIKE ME.
I'VE NEVER SEEN TOMOE OVERSLEEP.
HE ALREADY GETS BETTER GRADES THAN I DO.
HE DOES HIS SHRINE DUTIES AND THE HOUSEWORK PERFECTLY. HE'S ALSO GOOD WITH GIRLS...

WHERE ARE YOU, NANAMI?
THAT'S WHY ...
TOMOE ...
...I FEEL SO SECURE...
...WHEN TOMOE IS WITH ME.
TOMOE...
THERE'S NOTHING...
...TOMOE CAN'T DO.

BAM
NANAMI!
NANAMI...
TOMOE...

TOMOE
?
ARE YOU ALL RIGHT? NANAMI!
I'LL GET YOU OUT OF HERE RIGHT AWAY.
TOMOE
...

TOMOE...
...OPEN YOUR EYES.
PLEASE ...
PULL YOURSELF TOGETHER!
YOU'RE COLD...
NANAMI!

DON'T ...
...LEAVE ME BEHIND!
IS TOMOE'S VOICE...
...TREM-BLING?

AH...
IT'S MY FAULT...
...THAT TOMOE...
...LOOKS SO SAD...
I'VE MADE HIM WORRY ABOUT ME...
SORRY ...
... TOMOE ...

COME WITH ME...
...MASTER FOX.
WE'LL SAVE...
...THAT GIRL.
I PROMISED...
...I'D...
...MARRY TOMOE...

HER BODY'S COLD.
CAN WE WARM HER UP SOME-HOW?
HER BODY IS FINE...
...BUT HER SOUL IS FREEZING.
SHE'LL BE FINE IF SHE DRINKS THIS MEDICINE.
MEDI-CINE?
WHAT SORT OF MEDICINE ?
YOU BETTER NOT BE PLANNING TO POISON HER.

THAT GIRL GOT BACK OUR DRAGON KAMI'S ROBE OF FEATHERS.
NOW UNARI'S ANGER WILL BE QUELLED AND THIS STORM WILL CEASE.
WE OWE THAT GIRL.
WE CAN'T LET HER DIE.
WHO THE HELL WERE THOSE GUYS ANYWAY?
DON'T KNOW. BUT THEY SNUCK INTO UNARI'S HOME AND STOLE HER ROBE.
HMPH.
I SHOULD'VE KILLED ALL OF THEM.

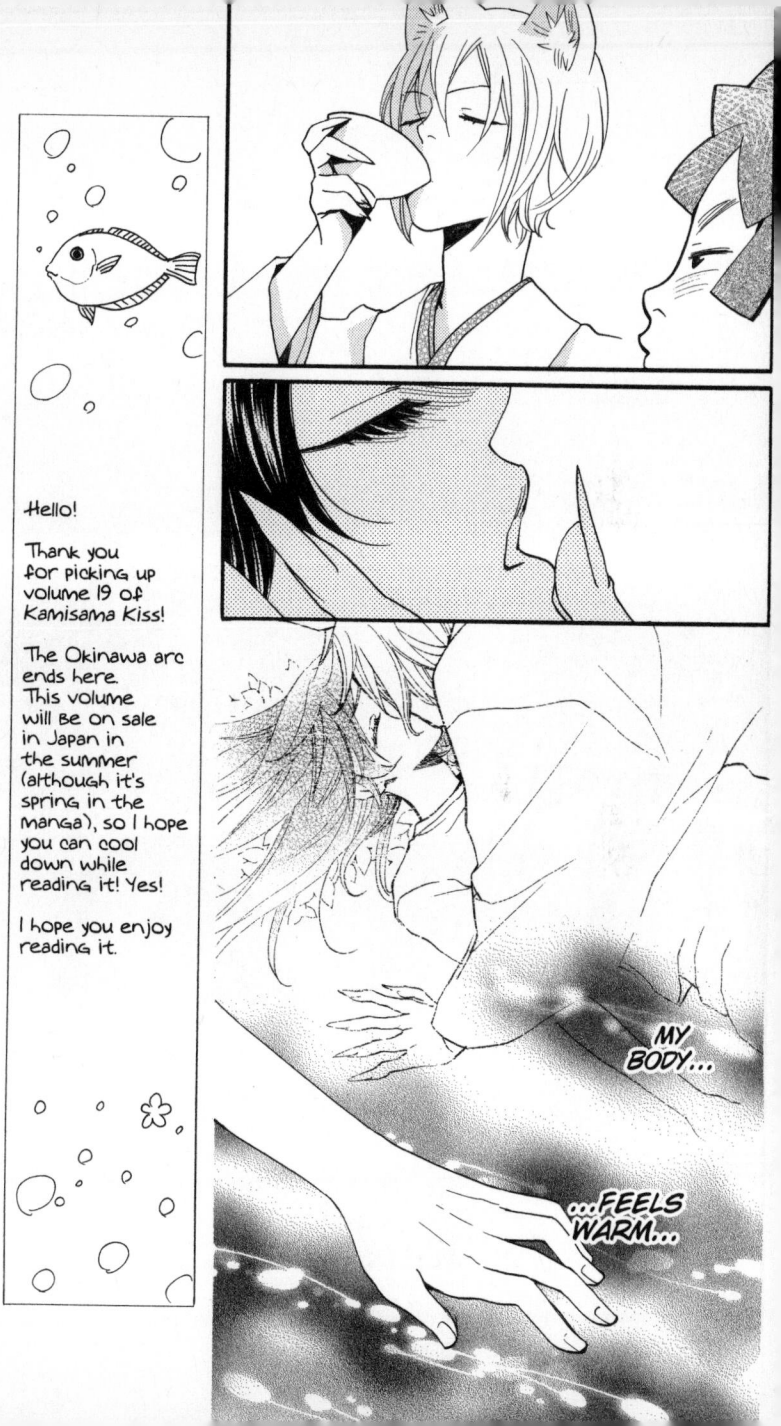
Hello!
Thank you for picking up volume 19 of Kamisama Kiss!
The Okinawa arc ends here. This volume will be on sale in Japan in the summer (although it's spring in the manga), so I hope you can cool down while reading it! Yes!
I hope you enjoy reading it.
MY BODY...
...FEELS WARM...

I FEEL NICE...
...AND WARM...
ARE YOU AWAKE, NANAMI?
...
TOMOE?

WHERE AM I?
IT'S SAFE HERE. REST FOR A WHILE.
HOW COULD YOU BE SO RECKLESS?
UGH...
I'M SORRY ...
NO NEED TO CRY.

I'M SORRY ...
YOU'RE ALIVE. THAT'S ENOUGH.

JUST THINK BEFORE YOU ACT NEXT TIME.
I FEEL SAFE WHEN I'M WITH TOMOE.
TOMOE MUST FEEL THE SAME WAY ABOUT ME.
WE NEED EACH OTHER.

WE SUPPORT EACH OTHER.
BECOMING HIS WIFE...
BEING WITH HIM...
NOW I KNOW WHAT THAT REALLY MEANS.

I GOTTA TELL HIM.
I'M SORRY.
I GOTTA TELL HIM...
...THE TRUTH...
YOU DON'T NEED TO APOLOGIZE.
THERE'S SOMETHING...
...I'VE BEEN WANTING TO TELL YOU.
HMM?
YOU'RE HOARSE.
YOU WANT SOME WATER?
UM...
I...
YEAH.

...KISSED KIRIHITO BY ACCIDENT...
I'M SORRY...
NO NEED TO WORRY...
...SINCE YOU'RE ALIVE.
I SHOULD'VE TOLD HIM EARLIER.

TOMOE STROKED MY HEAD GENTLY.
I FELT SO COMFORTABLE ...
...AND RELIEVED...
...THAT I...
...FELL INTO A DEEP SLEEP AGAIN.
I'LL REALLY DO MY BEST...
...WHEN I RECOVER AND WAKE UP.

SO WAIT FOR ME...
WAIT!
MASTER FOX?
KIRIHITO IS...
...THAT BRAT IN BLACK I MET IN THE LAND OF THE DEAD.
HMPH...

I REALLY SHOULD'VE KILLED HIM...
...ON THE SPOT...
The storm is raging.
The first day in Okinawa is about to end.

And the second day in Okinawa begins.

Kamisama Kiss
Chapter 109

FWOOOO
WELL, WELL.
THE STORM'S STILL RAGING...
I GUESS WE'LL STAY IN THE HOTEL FOR ANOTHER DAY.
WELL.
I DON'T CARE WHERE I AM AS LONG AS I CAN RELAX.
FWOOSH
TENGU-KUN!

SORRY I KEPT YOU WAITING! I FINALLY HEARD FROM MY BRETHREN!
NOW I KNOW WHERE UNARI LIVES!
SO GET READY AND WE'LL GO TOGETHER!
WAH...
WAH...
WOW... WE REALLY GOT HERE.
IS THIS LIKE A DIMENSIONAL PATHWAY?
EXCUSE ME...
...BUT YOU YOKAI SHOULD TAKE CARE OF YOUR OWN PROBLEMS.
THERE'S NOTHING A HUMAN LIKE ME CAN—
UNARI LIVES IN A CAVE ON THE SOUTHERN SEABED.
RATTLE
WILL YOU LISTEN TO ME?!

IF YOU'RE AN IDOL, EARN THOSE CDS WITH YOUR BODY!
WHA!
...BUT AMI ...
...ALWAYS BUYS YOUR CDS THE DAY THEY'RE RELEASED.
I DON'T CARE WHETHER YOU'RE A HUMAN OR A YOKAI ...
WHA!
ALL RIGHT, ALL RIGHT.
I KNOW SOMEONE WHO KNOWS A MOUNTAIN HERMIT IN KYOTO.
I'LL ASK HIM...
TOSS
YOU'RE SUCH A PAIN TO DEAL WITH.
GRAB
HELLO
...TO LIGHT A SACRED FIRE AND SAY A PRAYER.

Y...
YOU SNAKE!
YOU'LL FALL IF YOU DON'T FLY.
FLAP
YOU ...
HOW COULD YOU DO THIS?
...IDIOT SNAKE!
TCH.
SO HE'S A YOKAI TOO.

WHAM
HERE.
TAKE AMI'S CLOTHES WITH YOU.
IF YOU DON'T BRING AMI BACK...
...I'LL LEAK WHAT YOU REALLY ARE TO THE PRESS.

NOW LET'S GO, TENGU-KUN!
TO UNARI'S SEABED CAVE!
WHY?
WHY'S THIS HAPPENING TO ME...?
CHOMP CHOMP

SWF
THIS GRASS TASTES DELICIOUS.
I'VE EATEN ALL OF IT.
OH?
WHAT AM I DOING HERE?
I WANT SOME MORE.
NOW I REMEMBER.
I CAME TO OKINAWA ON A SCHOOL TRIP...
...AND WAS TRANSFORMED INTO A DUGONG!
AND, AND...
HO HO HO.

EEK!
I'm scared!
YOU HAVE NOTHING TO FEAR.
YOUR BRAIN IS TURNING INTO A DUGONG'S.
YOU'LL BECOME ONE OF US IN A FEW HOURS.
I'M TURNING INTO A DUGONG?
YES, YOU ARE.
HOW ARE YOU FEELING, HUMAN GIRL?
YOUR BRAIN MUST BE ABOUT TO MELT AWAY.

HERE.
THIS SEA-WEED IS FOR YOU.
TOSS
SEA-WEED!
SEA-WEED!
HO HO HO.
THIS IS DELI-CIOUS.
THIS GRASS IS DELI-CIOUS!
SOON YOU'LL BE FREE FROM ALL SORTS OF WORRIES.
YOU'RE SUCH A FORTUNATE HUMAN GIRL...
SO I...

I WANT TO SEE HIM.

THIS PLACE IS LIKE A MAZE.
WE'LL EASILY GET LOST.
WAIT, SNAKE.
SHAKE SHIVER
IT'S DANGEROUS GOING OFF ALONE...
WHY'RE YOU SHAKING?
TUG
I GREW UP IN THE MOUNTAINS ...
...SO I HATE THIS SORT OF PLACE!
THEN LET'S FINISH OUR BUSINESS QUICKLY AND GO HOME.
DARN... HE'S USELESS.
I WANT TO SEE HIM...
...BEFORE I TURN INTO A FISH...

WE ALREADY EXPLAINED WHAT'S GOING ON.
WHY DO I NEED TO DO THAT?
USE A YOKAI SPELL AND MAKE HER THINK IT WAS ALL A DREAM.
AND SHUT THAT WOMAN UP WHEN WE RETURN.
Yeah!
YOU DON'T KNOW ANYTHING ABOUT HUMANS!
ONCE THEY GRADUATE, THEY'LL START BLABBING WHEN THEY'RE DRUNK!
AND WE MADE HER PROMISE SHE WON'T TELL ANY-ONE.
NANAMI-CHAN WON'T HAVE TO HIDE ANYTHING FROM THEM ANYMORE.
...EVEN THOUGH YOU LIVE AMONG THEM.
YOU DON'T TRUST HUMANS AT ALL...
THEY'RE NANAMI-CHAN'S FRIENDS. WE CAN TRUST THEM.

WHY DO YOU TRUST HUMANS?
I TRUST NANAMI-CHAN. ♡
SO I CAN TRUST OTHER HUMANS TOO.
ISN'T IT DIFFICULT LIVING IN THE HUMAN WORLD WHILE CONCEALING YOUR REAL IDENTITY?
YOU DON'T SEEM TO LIKE HUMANS ANYWAY.
IF YOU INTEND TO KEEP LIVING IN THE HUMAN WORLD...
...YOU SHOULD HAVE A HUMAN CLOSE TO YOU WHO KNOWS YOUR TRUE SELF.
YOU NEED SOMEONE WHO ACCEPTS YOU AS YOU ARE.
LIKE NANAMI-CHAN ACCEPTED ME. ♡

NO THANKS.
TMP TMP
WHY NOT?! IS IT BECAUSE YOU'RE A TENGU?!
HUMANS DON'T THINK MUCH OF TENGU!
THEY LIKE ME, THOUGH!
THAT'S NOT WHY.
BEING A TENGU AND GROWING UP IN MOUNT KURAMA...
THEY'RE BOTH ESSENTIAL PARTS OF ME.
THAT'S WHY...
...I DON'T WANT EVERYONE TO KNOW ABOUT IT...

...
WHAT'S THAT SOUND?
RUMBLE
RUMBLE
BOOM
TH...
THAT'S SEA-WATER!
...
TENGU-KUN...
WAS HE SWEPT AWAY?

It's getting hot.

I started walking outside every season this year because I want to do something good for my health. Nowadays it's difficult to go out while the weather's nice because it starts raining suddenly, or thunder starts to rumble.

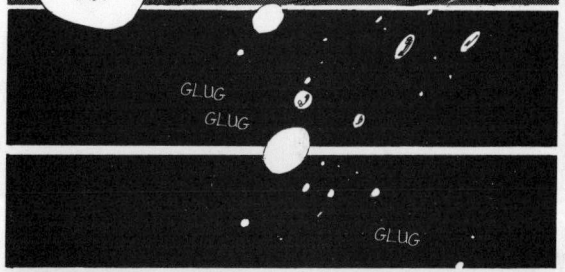

AM I...
...ALONE ?
SHIVER
SHIVER
DARN.
I CAN'T MOVE CUZ I FEEL ALL WEAK...
I JUST ...
THE ONLY ONES WHO CAN STAY CALM HERE...
...HAVE NERVES OF STEEL OR NO BRAINS AT ALL.
THE SEA IS DARK AND SPOOKY.
IT HASN'T CHANGED SINCE ANCIENT TIMES.
THIS IS A WORLD OF SILENCE AND DARKNESS.

TO COME HERE...
I DIDN'T HAVE TO COME HERE.
HMM?
WAAAH!

PEEP
PEEP
PEEP
...
S
W
F
...
ARE YOU A MANA-TEE?
NO, YOU'RE A DUGONG ...
...
AH...

...
WHAT'S WITH YOU...?
YOU'RE PRETTY FRIENDLY ...

THE DUGONG'S BODY...
...IS WARM...
THIS IS STRANGE.
I FEEL...

...JUST A LITTLE BIT...
...SAFER NOW THAT YOU'RE BY MY SIDE...
BE GOOD AND STAY HERE...
THE SEA IS STILL DARK, DEEP AND COLD.
I'M TERRIFIED OF THIS PLACE...
...BUT IT MUST BE PARADISE FOR YOU...

LIVING IN THE HUMAN WORLD IS LIKE BEING IN THE SEA.
I MADE UP MY MIND THAT I'D LIVE IN THE WATER ...
...SO I LEARNED TO BREATHE USING MY GILLS...
...AND BECAME GOOD AT ACTING LIKE A FISH.

BUT THE REAL ME...
...LOVES FLYING IN THE SKIES.

HEY.
TUG
...BUT I'M SO PATHETIC I GOT SWEPT AWAY...
DID YOU SEE A TOCHIGAMI NAMED NANAMI?
A HUMAN GIRL NAMED AMI WAS CAPTURED BY UNARI.
SWF
HEY.
WHERE'RE YOU GOING ...?
IS THIS DUGONG...
WE CAME TO RESCUE THEM...

...TAKING ME TO THEM?
SPLASH
...
PANT
THANKS...
...FOR BRINGING ME...
...HERE.
SO THIS IS WHERE UNARI LIVES...

HEY—
WHAT'S WRONG WITH ME?
MY STOMACH...
...HURTS SO MUCH.
NO.

THIS ISN'T MY STOMACH.
MY HEART FEELS TIGHT.
THIS IS MY HEART.
WHAT'S WRONG WITH ME?
WHY...
...AM I CRYING?
Kurama.
Kurama.

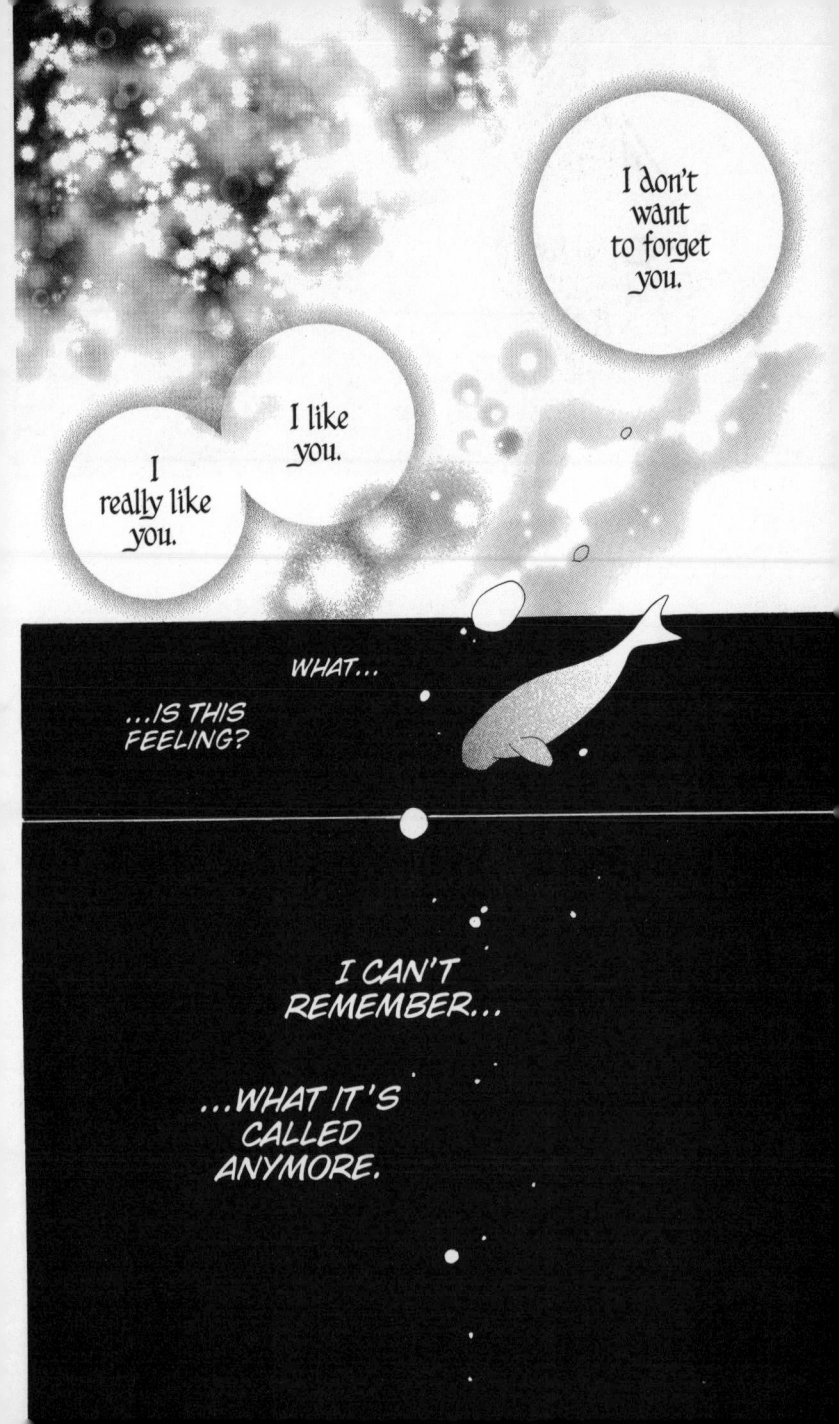
I don't want to forget you.
I like you.
I really like you.
WHAT...
...IS THIS FEELING?
I CAN'T REMEMBER...
...WHAT IT'S CALLED ANYMORE.

Kamisama Kiss
Chapter 110
HAPPY 6TH ANNIVERSARY!

SHEESH.
THIS SUCKS...
THIS PLACE IS BUMPY AND THERE'RE PUDDLES EVERYWHERE.
NANAMI-CHAN SHOULD BE HERE LOOKING FOR AMI...
DOES UNARI REALLY LIVE HERE?
...BUT I DON'T SENSE HER PRESENCE AT ALL.
PEEP PEEP
I'M DRENCHED WITH SEA-WATER...
...CUZ I HAVE TO SWIM BETWEEN GROTTOS.
I DON'T THINK I CAN COUNT ON THE TENGU-KUN...

...SO I GOTTA DO MY BEST.
I'LL RESCUE AMI...
...PUNISH UNARI...
...MAKE THE STORM STOP...
...AND CONTINUE MY SCHOOL TRIP WITH NANAMI-CHAN.
MIZUKI.
WERE YOU ABLE TO MEET UP WITH TOMOE-KUN?
I...
...MISS YOU.
NANAMI-CHAN.

FWOOSH
I'LL DO ALL I CAN...
...SO WAIT FOR ME, NANAMI-CHAN.
MASTER FOX,
HOW'S THE GIRL DOING?
AH.
SHE'S A LOT BETTER NOW.

MASTER FOX...
WHAT DO YOU MEAN?
DON'T YOU DARE DO ANYTHING INDECENT IN OUR HOME.
WE'RE HEADING FOR UNARI'S PLACE TO RETURN HER ROBE OF FEATHERS.
WHY DON'T YOU COME WITH US?
ZZZ
NO.
WELL FINE.
YOU TWO STAY HERE UNTIL THE STORM STOPS.
I HOPE UNARI QUELL'S HER ANGER WHEN SHE GETS HER ROBE BACK...
MMM
MMM
I'LL STAY WITH NANAMI...
...UNTIL SHE WAKES UP.

YOU SEEM TO BE TERRIFIED OF UNARI.
IS SHE THAT HARD TO DEAL WITH?
UNARI'S THE GUARD WHO PROTECTS THE SEA...
...SO SHE SHOWS NO MERCY TOWARDS THOSE WHO DISRUPT THE PEACE.
A LONG TIME AGO...
...A GIANT SPIRIT FISH WAS SWEPT AWAY FROM THE EASTERN SEA...
...AND STRANDED HERE.
BOOO
HOO
THE SPIRIT FISH CRIED AND ASKED US TO RETURN IT TO THE SEA...
IT WAS SO HUGE, NO ONE COULD DO ANYTHING ABOUT IT.
...BUT UNARI...

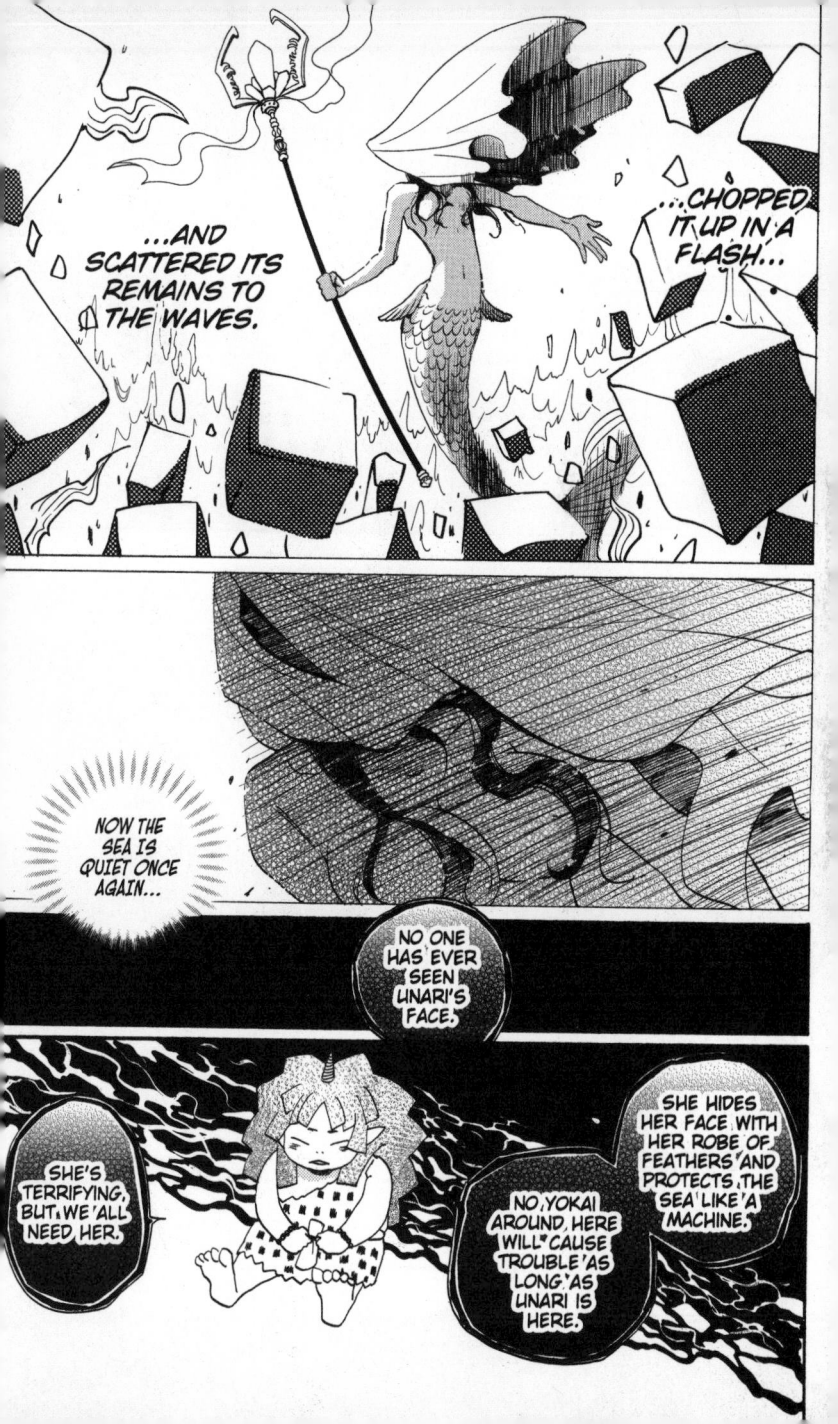
...AND SCATTERED ITS REMAINS TO THE WAVES.
...CHOPPED IT UP IN A FLASH...
NOW THE SEA IS QUIET ONCE AGAIN...
NO ONE HAS EVER SEEN UNARI'S FACE.
SHE'S TERRIFYING, BUT WE ALL NEED HER.
NO YOKAI AROUND HERE WILL CAUSE TROUBLE AS LONG AS UNARI IS HERE.
SHE HIDES HER FACE WITH HER ROBE OF FEATHERS AND PROTECTS THE SEA LIKE A MACHINE.

NOW UNARI HERSELF IS DISTURBING THE PEACE OF THE SEA.
IF WE DON'T STOP HER QUICK...
...THE BALANCE ...
...BETWEEN THE SEA AND THE ISLANDS WILL BE DESTROYED.
I SEE.
SO THE IRON LADY IS HAVING A FIT.

WHY DID I HAVE TO COME HERE ALONE...?
GLOOM
...
CLATTER
CLATTER
CLATTER
I CAME IN HERE WITHOUT THINKING IT THROUGH ...
WHAT SHOULD I DO ...?
WHERE'S THE SNAKE, FOX AND NANAMI?
WHERE THE HELL AM I?!
SO WHAT DO I DO WHEN I SEE THIS UNARI YOKAI?
WILL SHE LISTEN TO ME WHEN I DON'T EVEN HAVE HER ROBE WITH ME?

SZORU
MROZ-UP
SOME-ONE'S SNOR-ING?
SNORE
FWIP
SNORE
SNORE

THIS ...
...IS UNARI?!
SNORE

IS SHE ASLEEP?
SNAP

SHOVE
YOU SAW...
...MY FACE ...
WHA?
WHO ARE YOU, INTER-LOPER ...?!
I'M A FRIEND OF NANAMI, THE HUMAN KAMI WHO CAME TO SEE YOU.
I'M NOT YOUR ENEMY.
I ONLY WANT YOU TO FREE AMI, THE GIRL YOU'VE CAPTURED...
THAT GIRL IS SWIMMING HAPPILY INSIDE THIS CAVE...
...BECAUSE SHE'S NO LONGER HUMAN.
HUH ?

HER BRAIN WILL DEVOLVE AS TIME PASSES...
...AND SHE WON'T KNOW WHO SHE IS ANYMORE.
I TRANSFORMED HER INTO A DUGONG SO SHE'LL BE COMFORTABLE HERE.
AMI.
HA HA ...
SO THAT DUGONG WAS HER.
THAT'S WHY SHE WAS SO FRIENDLY.
BUT I CAN'T TAKE HER BACK IN THAT FORM.
TRANSFORM HER BACK INTO A HUMAN—
!
GRAB
SHAAH!

ATTACKING ME IN MY SLEEP CANNOT BE HOW HUMANS ASK FOR HELP THESE DAYS.
CLENCH
YOU DEFILED MY BEDROOM WITH YOUR SHOD FEET.
SQUEEZE
THAT MEANS YOU'VE COME TO KILL ME!
O...
OF COURSE NOT.
I'D NEVER ATTACK A WOMAN ...
...WHILE SHE'S ASLEEP ...

I THOUGHT SHE WAS GONNA BREAK MY ARMS!
SHE'S UNBELIEV-ABLY STRONG!
YOU'RE THE SECOND MAN...
...WHO HAS SEEN ME...
...AS A WOMAN.
THE FIRST ONE DECEIVED ME...
...STOLE MY ROBE OF FEATHERS AND RAN AWAY.
GRR
GRRR

I started to turn the air conditioner on since it's getting hot, but then day by day I started to get sick. I couldn't figure out what was happening, but I then found out my body was getting cold internally because of the air conditioner. What a surprise.

"Being cold" and "getting cold internally" are different...!

Drinking ginger tea warmed me up.

Everyone watch out for summer fatigue!

GRAB
I SEE.
YOU WISH TO MAKE ME YOUR WIFE.
I WILL ONLY ...
...SHOW MY FACE...
...TO THE MAN WHO WILL BE MY HUSBAND.
YOU'RE THE SECOND MAN WHO'S SEEN MY FACE.
NO... HOLD IT.
I'M NOT ASKING YOU TO MARRY ME—
WAAAH!

THE FIRST ONE...
...STOLE MY ROBE OF FEATHERS AND HASN'T YET RETURNED.
NOW.
LIFT MY VEIL...
YOU WILL NOT...
...BETRAY ME. WILL YOU?
...AND KISS THE LIPS OF THE WOMAN WHO WILL BE YOUR WIFE.

IT'LL BE DIFFICULT TO STAY IN THE WATER IN THIS FORM...
...SINCE I DON'T HAVE A BEAUTIFUL TAIL AND FINS LIKE YOURS.
...I'LL NEED TO BECOME A MERMAID.
IF I'M GONNA BE YOUR HUS-BAND ...
NOT TO WORRY.
EVERY LIVING BEING IN THIS WORLD WAS BORN FROM THE SEA.
BEASTS WHO GROVEL ON THE LAND. BIRDS WHO FLY THE SKIES.
IF YOU DRINK THIS WATER OF EVOLUTION ...
...YOU WILL FIRST DEVOLVE TO THE SOURCE BEING AND THEN EVOLVE INTO ANY LIFE-FORM YOU DESIRE.

FROM THOSE OF THE SEA INTO THOSE OF THE LAND.
FROM THOSE OF THE SKIES INTO THOSE OF THE SEA ...
HERE, MY FUTURE HUSBAND.
DRINK THIS WATER AND BECOME ONE OF US.
IF I DRINK THIS WATER ...
...WILL I BE ABLE TO BECOME A DUGONG TOO?

ANY LIFE-FORM I DESIRE...
OF COURSE. BUT DON'T DO THAT.
I CANNOT HAVE MY FUTURE HUSBAND...
...TRANS-FORM INTO SUCH A CREATURE.
...A DUGONG CAN TRANSFORM BACK INTO A HUMAN...
THAT MEANS...
...RIGHT?

FLAP
...I CAN LEAVE THIS STUFFY PLACE!
NOW THAT I HAVE THIS WATER...

SORRY. SAVE YOUR PRECIOUS KISS FOR YOUR FUTURE HUSBAND.
YOU...
...DE-CEIVED ME!
OOPS.
WHIZ
YOU BAS-TARD!
BAM
BA BAM
YOU CAN'T HIT ME.
NO WAY A FISH CAN BEAT ME...

RUMBLE
Is this the sound of-
...IN A DOGFIGHT ...
OH?
BOOM
WHO ARE YOU?
WHAT'S YOUR FIRST NAME?

I CAN'T...
AMI.
...LEAVE HER SWIMMING ALONE...
...IN THIS COLD SEA.
YOU CANNOT ESCAPE FROM ME.

WE'RE AT THE BOTTOM OF THE SEA.
THERE ARE ONLY THE TWO OF US HERE.
YOU CAN MAKE THIS SEA YOURS IF YOU BECOME MY HUSBAND.
SO WHY DO YOU NEED TO WORRY...
...ABOUT A MERE HUMAN GIRL?!
I THINK ...
...I CARE ABOUT HER.

IF YOU WON'T BE MINE...
HE APPROACHED ME WHEN HE DIDN'T EVEN LOVE ME.
I'LL KILL THE FIRST MAN AS WELL..
GAK
Wah!
HE FORCED HIMSELF ...
...DIE!

HE WILL PAY DEARLY FOR IT!
...INTO MY HEART.
BOTH OF YOU DISTURBED THE PEACE OF THIS SEA!
THE SEA...
...WILL NO LONGER BE PEACEFUL!
BOTH OF YOU VIOLATED MY HEART!
GAK

DOES THAT MEAN THIS STORM WON'T STOP?
ARE YOU UNARI-SAN?
I'VE BEEN LOOKING ALL OVER FOR YOU. ★
YOU SHOULD'VE GOTTEN HERE FASTER...
Mizuki arrives.

Kamisama Kiss
Chapter 111

I MADE UP MY MIND THE DAY MOM AND I LEFT OUR OLD HOME...
...THAT I'D NEVER LET ANYBODY TOUCH ME AGAIN.
BUT I REALLY MIGHT'VE BEEN WAITING...
...FOR SOMEONE TO OPEN THIS HEAVY DOOR INSIDE ME.

UNARI.
UNARI.
MOMMY.
YOU'D HAVE BECOME A BEAUTIFUL MERMAID IF YOU'D ONLY INHERITED MY BLOOD...
...BUT YOU INHERITED YOUR FATHER'S DRAGON CLAN LOOKS.
UGLY HORNS LIKE THESE DON'T GROW ON MERMAIDS.
I CAN'T TAKE YOU TO THE PARTY...
POOR UNARI.
...BECAUSE YOU'RE UGLY...
WON'T YOU TAKE ME TO THE PARTY IF I WEAR THIS?
LOOK, MOMMY. I MADE A HAIR ORNAMENT FROM SEASHELLS.
UNARI.

SHP
POOR UNARI...
IF YOU REALLY WANT TO GO TO THE PARTY...
...WEAR THIS ROBE OF FEATHERS.
NO ONE CAN HURT YOU...
...AS LONG AS YOU WEAR THIS.
SNAP
SOMEDAY A MAN WILL SURELY APPEAR.
SOMEONE WHO'LL FIND YOU LOVELY DESPITE YOUR UGLINESS...
SOME-DAY.

AT LEAST ONE MAN...
UNARI.
I HEARD YOU'RE ANGRY BECAUSE SOMEONE STOLE YOUR PRECIOUS ROBE OF FEATHERS.
I'M SORRY.
WE WANT TO DO EVERYTHING WE CAN TO GET YOUR ROBE BACK...
...SO WILL YOU QUELL YOUR ANGER AND STOP THIS STORM?
IT WILL REALLY INCONVENIENCE ME IF THIS STORM DOESN'T GO AWAY.

FWIP
I SIMPLY FOLLOWED THE PATHS HERE.
JERK!
YOU'RE LATE! WHAT WERE YOU DOING ?!
SO WHERE'S NANAMI-CHAN?
SHE'S NOT HERE.
PROMISES DISAPPEAR ...
IF NANAMI-CHAN PROMISED YOU, WE'RE FINE.
SHE PROMISED TO GET MY ROBE BACK IN EXCHANGE FOR THE HOSTAGE. SHE RETURNED ABOVE GROUND BUT STILL HASN'T COME BACK...
YOUR ROBE WILL COME BACK SOON.
...LIKE BUBBLES!

WHY NOT?
BECAUSE ...
LOOM
AND IT'S TOO LATE ANYWAY.
MY HEART WILL NOT QUIET DOWN EVEN IF MY ROBE COMES BACK.
NOT EVEN ONE MAN...
...NO ONE LOVES ME.
I GET IT.
THE ONLY ONES WHO APPROACH ME HAVE ULTERIOR MOTIVES LIKE THAT MAN OVER THERE!
NOBODY TRIES TO GET CLOSE TO MY HEART.
EVERYONE'S FRIGHTENED OF ME!

YOU'RE ALL ALONE AND FEEL...
...ISO-LATED.
I'LL STOP THIS STORM IF THAT LIAR BECOMES MY HUSBAND AND STAYS HERE.
JOLT
NOW ANSWER ME!
I WON'T LET YOU MARRY THE TENGU-KUN.
HOW ABOUT I BECOME YOUR HUSBAND INSTEAD?

FEELING EDGY AND NOT BEING ABLE TO MAKE IT GO AWAY.
UNBEARABLE LONELINESS.
YOU IDIOT!
WHAT ARE YOU SAYING!
She'll kill you!
I'VE EXPERIENCED THOSE FEELINGS TOO...
...BUT NANAMI-CHAN SAVED ME.
UNARI...
SO LET ME FIRST SAY THIS...
I WON'T LIE LIKE THIS TENGU-KUN DID.
BESIDES, NANAMI-CHAN'S SCHOOL TRIP WILL BE RUINED IF WE DON'T STOP THIS STORM.

IF YOU DON'T MIND THAT...
UGH!
UGH!
NANAMI-CHAN IS THE MOST IMPORTANT TO ME.
THAT WILL NEVER CHANGE.
...I'LL STAND AS CANDIDATE ...
...FOR YOUR HUSBAND.
SOMEONE IS HOLDING ME...
...FOR THE VERY FIRST TIME...
I've warned you!
Don't blame me if something happens!

FWOOSH
FWOOSH
...
YOU MAY LEAVE NOW.
...
Y...
YOU GIVE AMI BACK!
I DON'T NEED THAT GIRL ANY-MORE.
I'VE ALREADY RELEASED HER.
SHE MUST BE SWIMMING FREELY IN THE OPEN SEA.
IN THE OPEN SEA?!
TENGU-KUN.

I recently felt that humans can't live unless they love something or someone.

I hope everyone's lives are filled with love.

TAKE CARE OF AMI.

I CAN'T DO MUCH OF ANYTHING.

I CAN'T LOOK AFTER YOKAI.

I DON'T CARE WHAT HAPPENS TO YOU ...

...SO YOU BETTER TAKE CARE, YOUR-SELF!

I'M NOT LIKE THEM.
I CAN BARELY SAVE ONE HUMAN BEING.
HER BRAIN WILL DEVOLVE AS TIME PASSES...
...AND SHE WON'T KNOW WHO SHE IS ANYMORE.
I'VE GOTTA MAKE HER DRINK THIS QUICK AND TURN HER BACK INTO A HUMAN.
FWOOOO
SO.
WHERE IN THE SEA IS SHE?
FWOO...
KA-SPLASH

UNARI.
I CAN'T FIND HER IN THIS ROUGH WATER...
STOP THIS STORM QUICK!
WHAT'S GOING ON HERE?
I HAVEN'T INTRO-DUCED MYSELF YET.
I'M MIZUKI.
I CAN'T STOP MY HEART ...
...FROM BEATING FAST.
AH, THIS IS GOOD.

SO WON'T YOU TELL ME MORE ABOUT YOUR-SELF?
WE ONLY KNOW EACH OTHER'S NAMES.
I'M JUST AS YOU SEE ME.
JUST AS I SEE YOU?
HOW AM I SUPPOSED TO LOOK AT YOU...
...WHEN YOU'RE HIDING BEHIND THAT CLOTH?
GRAB
!
DON'T LOOK AT ME!
NOW I KNOW YOU'RE THE SHY TYPE.
AH...

WHAT A BEAUTIFUL MAN.
HE REMINDS ME OF MOTHER.
CRUNCH CRUNCH
HOW WILL HE BE ABLE TO SIT CLOSE TO MY HEART?
HOW CAN SOMEONE LIKE HIM FALL IN LOVE WITH ME?
IF YOU DON'T WANT ME TO LOOK AT YOU...
AM I BEING DECEIVED...
...AGAIN?

FWIP
...I'LL WEAR THIS INSTEAD.
I DON'T MEAN TO DEFEND THE TENGU-KUN...
...BUT YOU LOOK SCARY WHEN YOU'RE WEARING THIS.
NO ONE CAN GET CLOSE TO YOU...
CRUNCH
CRUNCH
...CUZ YOU LOOK SUSPICIOUS.
BUT YOU'VE GOT SUCH BEAUTIFUL EYES.
BEAUTIFUL?
Uh
Uh
I MADE ...
...THOSE.
WHAT REALLY? AMAZING.
WHAT ARE THEY?
SALT-FLAVORED JELLYFISH BEANS.
ANY-THING ELSE?
TELL ME MORE ABOUT YOUR-SELF.

YOU'RE A GOOD COOK.
DID HE REALLY LOOK AT MY FACE WHEN HE SAID I'M BEAUTIFUL?
IS THIS MAN...
Salty
Hmm
LET ME TRY ONE.
CANDIED SALTED FERMENTED SQUID.
I ALSO MADE THIS.
CRUNCH
NO...
SHP
SHP
I'M GOOD AT MAKING SAKE, SO I'LL MAKE SOME FOR YOU.
...ANOTHER LIAR?
YET YOU SAID I'M BEAUTIFUL.
DID YOU REALLY MEAN WHAT YOU SAID?
I CAN'T BEAR SOME-ONE LYING TO ME ANY-MORE ...
NO ONE APPROACHES ME BECAUSE THEY'RE FRIGHTENED OF ME...
...AND BECAUSE I'M UGLY.
WHAT'S THE MATTER, UNARI?

YOU'RE BEAUTIFUL.
YEAH.
I THINK THEY'RE BEAUTIFUL.
YOUR EYES ARE CLEAR BLUE LIKE THE OKINAWAN SEA.
I BELIEVE YOUR WORDS!

HE'S THE ONE MAN WHO LOVES ME.
HE'S THE ONE!
I HAVE FINALLY MET HIM.
NOW WIND, GO TELL EVERYONE ...
...THAT UNARI AND MIZUKI WILL BECOME HUSBAND AND WIFE.
THE LONG, LONG WINTER IS OVER...
...AND SPRING...
...HAS COME FOR THE FIRST TIME.

I...
...was always alone...
?
AH.
...but I never felt lonely...
THE SEA...
...IS BECOMING QUIET.

WHAT'S GOING ON? WE HAVEN'T GIVEN HER ROBE BACK YET.
HMM.
UNARI IS SINGING.
SHE'S STOPPED BEING ANGRY.
IT SEEMS...
...THE SNAKE AND THE MERMAID ARE GETTING MARRIED.
Heh heh
G-GETTING MARRIED!?!
I'm not alone anymore...
...but I can't help feeling lonely...
...when I think of a world without you.

THE WAVES ARE QUIETING DOWN...
...BUT I'LL NEVER FIND HER BY SEARCHING BLINDLY.
AMI!
AMI NEKOTA!
COME OUT.
COME OUT OF THE SEA...
...QUICK...
A SONG?
IS THAT WOMAN...
...SINGING THIS SONG?

I MADE UP MY MIND THE DAY I LEFT HOME...
...THAT I'D NEVER GET INVOLVED WITH ANYBODY AGAIN.

BUT REALLY, I MIGHT'VE BEEN WAITING...
THE WATER IS WARM...
I FEEL LIKE I'VE FORGOTTEN SOMETHING ...
...BUT WHO CARES.
CHOMP CHOMP
...FOR SOMEONE TO OPEN THIS HEAVY DOOR...
...INSIDE ME.

WHERE ARE YOU...
...AMI?
I KNOW ...
...THIS SONG.
I CAN HEAR A SONG.
IT SOUNDS FAMILIAR FOR SOME REASON.
I LOVE...
...THIS SONG.
NOW I REMEMBER.

THE ONE I LIKE BEST...
...SINGS THIS SONG.

AMI!
I FOUND YOU!
I'VE FINALLY ...

...FOUND YOU.
CHOO
I SHOULD THANK YOUR FRIEND FOR GIVING ME THOSE CLOTHES.
ARE YOU FEELING ALL RIGHT?
SHE WAS NAKED... COMPLETELY NAKED ...
I'M SO GLAD I WAS CARRYING HER CHANGE OF CLOTHES!
...
I REMEMBER WE TALKED IN THE SEA...

...WHEN I WAS A FISH.
YOU SAID...
...YOU LOVE FLYING THE SKIES.
I COULDN'T SPEAK THEN...
...BUT THERE'S SOMETHING I'VE BEEN WANTING TO TELL YOU...
I...
...LIKE WATCHING YOU FLY THE SKIES.
I REALLY DO.

I THINK I'VE BEEN WAITING...
...FOR SOMEONE TO SAY THAT TO ME FOREVER.
...THE REAL ME.
YOU'VE TOUCHED...

MIZUKI AND UNARI...
...ARE GETTING MARRIED!
HEH.
I SHOULD CONGRATULATE HIM.
Kamisama Kiss
Chapter 112
SHOULDN'T YOU STOP HIM? HE'S ONE OF YOU.
UNARI MUST'VE CAPTURED HIM.
I GUESS.
Rip
Rip
HE PROBABLY BECAME A HOSTAGE IN PLACE OF AMI...
...BUT WHO CARES.

THAT SNAKE WAS ALWAYS IN MY WAY, BUT NOW HE'LL BE GONE FROM MIKAGE SHRINE.
HA HA HA HA HA HA
I'll gladly offer him to Unari!
No returns!
RISE
WHAT'S THIS ABOUT MIZUKI?
...
AAH...

WHICH COLOR DO YOU PREFER, PINK OR GREEN?
MY HUSBAND IS WATCHING ME.
HE'S NOT SCARED OF ME.
AND...
I'VE NEVER SEEN FISH LIKE THIS!
WAH! THIS IS AMAZ-ING.
I'M HAPPY.
HE'S GENTLE.
HE'S BEAUTIFUL.
HE DOESN'T TAKE ADVANTAGE OF ME.
SURE!
...HE SAYS HE LIKES ME.
THEN I'LL HAVE THE PINK ONE...
HO HO HO... SO WE'LL BE EATING THEM?

I'VE FINALLY FOUND MY SPOUSE!
MY DEAR HUS-BAND.
DO STAY WITH ME FOREVER.
I'M SO HAPPY!
SURE.
BECAUSE...
HO HO HO.
I'LL GO PICK SOME FLOWERS.
...I'LL NEVER BE ALONE AGAIN.
MY DEAR HUSBAND. DID YOU FIND SOME OCTOPUS ?
NEVER...
EVER...

...
HYA HYA HYA.
WHAT A SUR-PRISE!
ARE YOU UNARI ?

BLAST ...
I LEFT MY SPEAR BEHIND.
WHO ARE THEY?
ROGUES OF THE SEA.
SO THAT'S WHAT YOU LOOK LIKE!
FIRST TIME I'VE SEEN YOUR FACE!
WHAT'RE YOU GONNA DO ABOUT IT?
HUNH ?
UNARI.
ONE OF OUR BROTHERS WAS SWEPT AWAY BY THE TIDE THANKS TO YOUR WILD STORM!
YOUR HUS-BAND ?!
YES! DON'T HURT HIM!
STOP!
GET AWAY FROM MY HUS-BAND!
SHUT UP! WHO THE HELL ARE YOU ANYWAY ?!
THE TIDE WILL BRING HIM BACK EVENTUALLY.
!

Hya Hya Hya
SO THIS WIMP IS YOUR HUSBAND?!
!
I'LL BITE HIS HEAD OFF.
NO!
CHOMP
HOW DARE YOU MERE YOKAI SAY SUCH THINGS TO A SHINSHI?

FWOOSH
TOSS
SO ONE OF YOU WAS SWEPT AWAY BY THE TIDE?
GO GET HIM.
!!
!!
...
WHAT ARE YOU?!

ARE YOU ALL RIGHT?
SORRY I LET GO OF THE FISH.
I GOTTA GO FIND ANOTHER PINK ONE.
NOW, I REALIZE ...
...I DON'T KNOW ANYTHING ABOUT THIS MAN.
I WANT TO KNOW MORE...

FLAP
KU-RAMA ...
...ABOUT HIM.
RATTLE
AMI ?!

SQUEEZE
ARE YOU ALL RIGHT, AMI?!
I WAS SO WORRIED!
KEI ...
I'M SORRY I MADE YOU WORRY SO MUCH, KEI.
WHAT'S WITH YOUR HAIR...?
WELL... WHO CARES! I'M GLAD YOU'RE BACK!
Ueshima! You're in there, aren't you?
How's Nekota doing?!
Open this door!
The teachers are worried! You haven't even eaten breakfast...
BANG BANG
I DIDN'T KNOW WHAT TO DO...
...CUZ BOTH MOMOZONO AND YOU WERE GONE.

RU-RIKO.
WE MEET IN THE LOBBY AT TWO P.M...
...SO GET READY TO LEAVE.
A BIRD...
...NO, IT'S NOT...

KLAK KLIK KLAK

...SINCE YOU BROUGHT THAT HUGE CAMERA.

ARE YOU TAKING SPY PHOTOS AGAIN?

TAKE PHOTOS OF US INSTEAD...

NO.

SO WHAT DID YOU SHOOT? LET ME SEE.

I CAN'T GIVE THIS SCOOP AWAY FOR FREE.

MIZUKI AND UNARI ARE GETTING MARRIED?!
WHAT'S GOING ON?!
ALL SORTS OF THINGS HAPPENED WHILE YOU WERE SOUND ASLEEP.
THEN WHERE'S AMI?
THE HUMAN GIRL'S APPARENTLY BEEN RELEASED ...
...SO THIS MARRIAGE MUST BE LIKE AN EXCHANGE OF HOSTAGES.
WE'LL GO RESCUE THEM NOW ...
NO.
YOU REST HERE.
I'LL GO RETURN THE ROBE OF FEATHERS.

ON MY WAY THERE, I'LL SEE HOW THE SNAKE'S DOING.
NO THANKS.
I'LL GO RETURN THE ROBE MYSELF.
WILL YOU TAKE ME TO UNARI'S PLACE ONCE MORE?
Sure.
DO YOU INTEND TO WANDER OFF ALONE AGAIN?!
NO.
BECAUSE YOU'LL COME WITH ME, WON'T YOU?

WHOA.
SUNLIGHT REACHES DOWN HERE IN THE SHALLOWS.
THIS IS MY PRIVATE GREEN-HOUSE.
THIS IS A FABULOUS VIEW!
DO YOU LIKE IT?
I'M GLAD IT'S WARM HERE...
...CUZ I DON'T LIKE THE COLD.
I WASN'T WORRIED AT FIRST...
...BUT NOW I WATCH EVERYTHING...
...THIS MAN DOES.

HAVE I...
...WHEN HE HASN'T CHANGED AT ALL?
WHY AM I DOING THIS...
HAVE I CHANGED?
YOU SAID YOU'RE A SHINSHI.
SO THAT NANAMI GIRL IS YOUR MASTER?
SHINSHI ARE HOLY BEASTS THAT SERVE KAMI-SAMA.
YEAH.
HMM... SORT OF.
DO YOU MEAN LIKE THIS?
OKINAWAN LION STATUES

SHE'S MY MOST PRECIOUS ONE.
NOW I KNOW WHY...
YOU SAID YOU'RE FAMILIAR WITH THE EMOTIONS I WAS FEELING...
...I WANT TO KNOW...
...WHAT YOUR CORE IS MADE OF.
SO TELL ME...
...MORE ABOUT YOU.
THEN WHY DID YOU AGREE TO MARRY ME?

GRAB
YOU'VE BARELY RECOVERED.
THIS IS WHY I TOLD YOU TO STAY BEHIND.
Air
YOU CAN'T EVEN BREATHE UNDERWATER.
Ah.
YOU CAN'T EVEN TALK UNDERWATER.
HUMANS ARE SO INCONVENIENT.
Glug
Glug
Glug
Air
Glug
Glug
Glug
Glug
LOTS MORE...

HUMAN KAMI. HOW ABOUT YOU WAIT ABOVE?
HER GARDEN SHOULD BE SOMEWHERE AROUND HERE.
SORRY... I NEVER THOUGHT UNARI WOULD GO OFF ON A DATE...
SHAKE SHAK
...SO I'LL RETURN HER ROBE AND GET MIZUKI BACK!
Glug
Glug
I PROMISED UNARI I'D BRING BACK HER ROBE OF FEATHERS...
Glug
A SEA SNAKE?
SWF
I CAN'T UNDERSTAND WHAT YOU'RE SAYING BECAUSE OF THE BUBBLES.
TELL ME WHEN YOUR BAG'S EMPTY.
GNH

SO YOU'LL TAKE ME...
...TO MIZUKI...
I ONCE WAS ALONE AND LOST ALL HOPE, LIKE YOU DID.

THEN NANAMI-CHAN SAVED ME.
WHENEVER I THINK ABOUT NANAMI-CHAN...
...MY HEART IS FILLED WITH HAPPINESS.

I LIKE NANAMI-CHAN.
I LIKE THINKING ABOUT NANAMI-CHAN.
I'LL NEVER FALL INTO THE DARKNESS AGAIN...
...AS LONG AS NANAMI-CHAN CONTINUES TO SMILE.

I THOUGHT YOU MIGHT BE SAVED TOO...
JUST HAVING HER CALL MY NAME...
...IS ALL I NEED.
...IF SOMEONE LIKE HER LIVED IN YOUR HEART.
...SO I WANTED TO SAVE SOMEONE ELSE WHO'D FALLEN INTO A SIMILAR HOLE.
NANAMI-CHAN SAVED ME...

YOU'RE THE FIRST ONE WHO HAS SAID SUCH THINGS TO ME...
THIS IS THE FIRST TIME...
...TO UNDERSTAND ME...
...SOMEONE GOT CLOSE ENOUGH TO MY HEART...

MY HEART, FROZEN FOR SO LONG, IS MELTING.
I HAVE LIVED UNTIL NOW...
I'M SO HAPPY ...
THIS IS THE FIRST TIME I'VE HELD SOMEONE SO PRECIOUS.
THANK YOU...
...MIZUKI.

...SO I COULD MEET THIS MAN.

MIZUKI!
Glug
...IS SIMPLY AMAZING.

NANAMI-CHAN!
HERE'S YOUR ROBE OF FEATHERS, UNARI!
SO RETURN THE HOSTAGE LIKE YOU PROMISED!
HOW COULD SHE—

SO THIS GIRL...
...IS YOUR CORE.
THANK YOU, NANAMI-CHAN.
NOW GO ENJOY YOUR SCHOOL TRIP.
GLUG
!
WELL, WELL.
HOW COULD YOU LEAVE YOUR BAG OF AIR BEHIND?
YOU'RE SUCH A PAIN TO DEAL WITH.

SMOOCH

SO YOUR MOST PRECIOUS ONE ALREADY HAS SOMEONE ELSE...
WE'RE SO MUCH ALIKE...
...MIZUKI.

Kamisama Kiss
Chapter 113

KISS
HOW COULD YOU DO THAT IN PUBLIC ?!
SOB SOB
I COULDN'T STOP MYSELF. I THOUGHT YOU'D SUFFOCATE ...
TOMOE-KUN...
GRRRR GRR
HMM ?
HOW DARE YOU DO SUCH A THING IN FRONT OF ME?!
TODAY, TODAY...
RAH
...I WILL NOT FORGIVE YOU!
OH, IT'S MIZUKI-DONO, EX-SHINSHI.

SINCERE CONGRATULATIONS ON YOUR MARRIAGE.
NOW MIKAGE SHRINE WILL BE QUIET.
GRAPPLE
INDEED. I'LL HAVE NO REGRETS AFTER I FINISH YOU OFF.
HEY, YOU TWO.
STOP FIGHTING NOW!
FREEZE
...
CLENCH
UNARI ...
HERE'S YOUR ROBE LIKE I PROMISED.
NOW GIVE MIZUKI BACK.

IT CONCEALED MY FACE BEAUTIFULLY FOR A LONG TIME...
THIS ROBE OF FEATHERS IS DIFFERENT FROM OTHER CLOTH.
...BUT I DON'T NEED IT ANYMORE ...
...BE-CAUSE MIZUKI ...
...ACCEPTED ME.

MIZUKI.
THIS IS MY FAREWELL GIFT.
IT'LL PROTECT YOU FROM FIRE...
...AND GIVE YOU AN ADVANTAGE OVER THAT FOX.
WHAT?!
NOW GO...
...TO THE GIRL WHO'S MOST PRECIOUS TO YOU.
UNARI?

I JUST NEED TO KNOW YOU EXIST SOMEWHERE IN THIS WORLD.
I WANTED A SPOUSE WHO ACCEPTED ME...
...BUT IF WE ALWAYS NEED TO BE TOGETHER, THAT'S NO DIFFERENT FROM BEING ALONE.
I'LL NEVER FEEL LONELY AGAIN AS LONG AS I THINK OF MY DEAR ONE.
YOU MUST FEEL THE SAME WAY TOO, MIZUKI.
YEAH.
WE'RE THE SAME IN THAT SENSE.

FWOOSH
NOW GO...
...BEFORE I CHANGE MY MIND.
SHOVE
LINARI!
I'LL... COME AGAIN.
I'LL COME SEE YOU...
...ONCE A YEAR...
...ON THIS DAY.

THAT MAKES ME SO HAPPY.
I'LL BE WAITING FOR YOU, MIZUKI.

PANT
I FEEL LIKE I'VE DONE A LIFETIME'S WORTH OF SWIMMING.
PANT
PA
WE'RE FINALLY ...
...ON LAND ...
PANT
PANT
YOU'LL CATCH A COLD.
LET'S RETURN TO THE HOTEL RIGHT AWAY.
WHERE'S MIZUKI?
I THOUGHT I'D ASK MIZUKI...

Thank you for reading this far!

If you have any comments and thoughts about volume 19, do let me hear from you!

The address is...

Julietta Suzuki
c/o Shojo Beat
VIZ Media, LLC
P.O. Box 77010
San Francisco
CA 94107

I'll be waiting.

I hope we'll be able to meet again in the next volume...

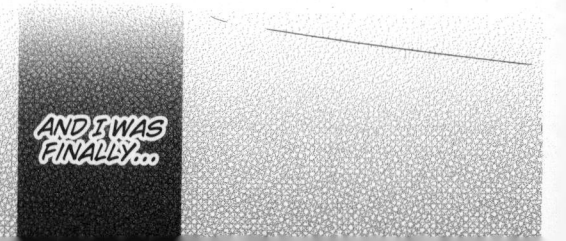

ARE YOU FEELING ALL RIGHT?
WHAT'S WITH YOUR HAIR?!
I'M FINE.
I'M SO GLAD YOU'RE ALIVE!
AMI!
...ABLE TO SEE...
...THE BLUE SKY OF OKINAWA.
NANAMI!
SHEESH.
AND I THOUGHT I WAS GONNA GET A STOMACH ULCER CUZ I WAS SO WORRIED.
I DON'T KNOW WHY...
...BUT I FEEL ENERGY GUSHING UP FROM INSIDE ME.
I WAS SO HUNGRY I ATE ALL OF KEI'S CHOCOLATES.

I...I'M SORRY, AMI.
I—
NANAMI, I ALREADY KNOW.
SHE DRANK THE WATER OF EVOLUTION ...
...SO FIRST SHE DEVOLVED AND THEN RE-EVOLVED INTO A HUMAN.
HER BODY'S BEEN RE-CREATED, SO OF COURSE IT'S DIFFERENT NOW.
WE DON'T HAVE MUCH TIME.
WE MEET IN THE LOBBY AT TWO P.M.
WHA ?
SO GET READY TO LEAVE.
AMI...
I DON'T CARE WHAT YOU ARE.
WE'RE STILL FRIENDS.

OUR SCHEDULE CHANGED CUZ THE STORM STOPPED.
WE'RE TAKING A BUS TO AN AQUARIUM.
THE HOTEL WILL SET OFF FIREWORKS AT DINNERTIME.
SO LET'S ENJOY OUR SCHOOL TRIP, NANAMI.
SHE'S RIGHT.
WE'RE IN OKINAWA...
...ON OUR SCHOOL TRIP!
YOU GO FIRST!
I'LL CHANGE AND COME RIGHT AWAY.
AN AQUARIUM! AN AQUARIUM!
I GOTTA HURRY ...
...AND HAVE FUN.

NO NEED TO HURRY...
...SINCE YOU'RE STAYING BEHIND.
HUH?
EVERYONE ALREADY THINKS YOU'RE SICK...
...SO I'LL TELL THE TEACHERS YOU'RE STILL NOT FEELING WELL.
WHA—

AMI'S FINE, BUT YOU'RE VERY ILL...
...SO GET SOME SLEEP.
MMM MMM.
YOU STAY HERE. YOU LOOK SO PALE.
Toss
IF YOU WANNA GO SOMEWHERE, TELL ME WHERE YOU'RE GOING, WHO YOU'RE GOING WITH, AND WHEN YOU'LL RETURN HOME.
DON'T DO ANYTHING RASH AGAIN WITHOUT MY PERMISSION.
NO! I'LL COME WITH YOU!
ONE MORE THING.
CALL ME WHAT YOU WANT.
WHAT THE HECK?! YOU'RE BEING SUCH A TYRANT!

YOU LET A STRANGE MAN TAKE ADVANTAGE OF YOU.
YOU THINK I'M NOT ANGRY ABOUT IT?
STAB
TAKEN ADVANTAGE OF...
...
I WON'T CHANGE MY MIND EVEN IF YOU MAKE THAT FACE.
NOW YOU'VE LEARNED YOUR LESSON. DON'T MEDDLE WHEN YOU CAN'T HANDLE IT YOURSELF.
W... WHERE'RE YOU GOING, TOMOE?

TO ENJOY MY SCHOOL TRIP.
I'LL HAVE FUN WHILE YOU STAY BEHIND.
BAM
VROOM
HELLO, STUDENTS OF UJIGAMI HIGH.
IT'S AN AMAZINGLY SUNNY DAY TODAY.
WE'RE HEADED FOR CHURAUMI AQUARIUM.
WAH
WAH
SO NANAMI'S STILL FEELING SICK...
AMI, YOU'RE EATING TOO MANY SWEETS.
I CAN'T STOP MYSELF.
OKINAWA

POOR NANAMI-CHAN.
SHE WAS SO LOOKING FORWARD TO THIS TRIP.
I KNOW ...
I'M ALONE IN THIS ROOM.
NOW THAT I'M BY MYSELF...
...I FEEL WEAK.
I WAS REALLY LOOKING FORWARD TO THIS SCHOOL TRIP...
I DON'T FEEL LIKE EATING...

...LOOKED LIKE AKURA-OH IN THAT MOMENT.

WHAT IS HE?

THIS IS A SCHOOL TRIP.
SO WHY DID I GET INTO THIS MESS...?
I WONDER IF TOMOE... IS HAVING FUN?
KA-CHAK
WE'RE HOME.
MOMO-ZONO. YOU AWAKE?
HEEEY...
ZZZ

WHAT TIME IS IT?
IT'S DARK ...
BOOM
BANG
TOMOE WAS RIGHT.
I FEEL A LOT BETTER...
...NOW THAT I'VE SLEPT FOR A WHILE.
F...
FIRE-WORKS!
BOOM
BOOM
I WAS VERY TIRED...
?
BOOM
BOOM
BOOM

NOW, I REMEMBER. THE HOTEL WAS GONNA SET OFF FIREWORKS AT DINNER-TIME.
RATTLE
BOOM
BOOM
SO EVERY-ONE'S BACK?
THEY SHOULD'VE WOKEN ME UP!
ALL RIGHT!
I'LL HAVE FUN TOMORROW!
YOU'RE BETTER NOW.
TOMOE.

THEY'RE WATCHING THE FIREWORKS DOWNSTAIRS.
WHY'RE YOU HERE?
WHERE'S EVERY-ONE?
IS THIS A KEY CHAIN?
HERE'S A SOU-VENIR FOR YOU.
HE'S RIGHT.
TOSS
It's Cute.
I'm surprised you picked something so cute!
OH, SHUT UP.
THEY SEEM TO BE HAVING FUN.

DID YOU HAVE FUN AT THE AQUARIUM ?
OTHER STUDENTS SEEMED TO BE HAVING FUN...
...BUT I DIDN'T ...
...CUZ YOU WEREN'T WITH ME.
HE'S BEING...
...SO ADORABLE...

"I'M HAPPY AS LONG AS I THINK OF MY DEAR ONE"...
WATER YOKAI ARE SO MATURE, LIKE HIMEMIKO.
BUT I NEED TO BE...
...WITH THE ONE I LOVE.
IS TOMOE BEING A LITTLE MORE HONEST THAN USUAL...
...BUT I FEEL HAPPY...
...EVEN THOUGH YOU LEFT ME BEHIND ...
YOU'RE BEING AWFULLY HONEST ...
...BECAUSE THIS ISN'T HOME?
I'M NOT QUITE SURE HOW TO RESPOND...

AS MY LOVE GROWS...
HEY...
CAN I HOLD YOU TIGHT?
I'M ALWAYS HONEST.
I ALWAYS EXPRESS MY LOVE FOR YOU.
DOES HE?
GRAB
GO AHEAD.
...WORDS JUST AREN'T ENOUGH.
I'M ALSO VERY HAPPY ...
...THAT YOU'RE WITHIN REACH.

UH OH...
THE FIREWORKS ARE BEAUTIFUL ...
...AND TOMOE LOOKS SO BEAUTIFUL IN THIS LIGHT.
I MIGHT REMEMBER THIS KISS FOR THE REST OF MY LIFE.

BOOM
BOOM
BOOM
BY THE WAY.
YOU DON'T MIND KISSING ME IN PUBLIC?
DON'T BE MEAN.
I DON'T MIND ...
...SINCE EVERYONE ELSE IS WATCHING THE FIRE-WORKS.
A LOT OF THINGS DIDN'T GO RIGHT ON THIS TRIP...

...BUT JUST BEING WITH TOMOE...
...MADE IT...
...WONDERFUL.
MIZUKI ?

WHAT ARE YOU DOING OUT HERE?
AREN'T YOU GONNA WATCH THE FIRE-WORKS?
I'M WATCH-ING.
I'M WATCHING THEIR REFLECTIONS IN THE SEA.
I FIND FIREWORKS TOO BRIGHT...
...SO IT'S BEST TO WATCH THEM ON THE SURFACE OF THE WAVES.

The Otherworld

Ayakashi **is an archaic term for yokai.**

Kami **are Shinto deities or spirits. The word can be used for a range of creatures, from nature spirits to strong and dangerous gods.**

Komainu **are a pair of guardian statues placed at the gate of a shrine, usually carved of stone. Depending on the shrine, they can be lions, foxes or cows.**

Onibi-warashi **are like will-o'-the-wisps.**

Shinshi **are birds, beasts, insects or fish that have a special relationship with a kami.**

Tengu **are a type of yokai. They are sometimes associated with excess pride.**

Tochigami **(or *jinushigami*) are deities of a specific area of land.**

Yokai **are demons, monsters or goblins.**

Honorifics

-chan **is a diminutive most often used with babies, children or teenage girls.**

-dono **roughly means "my lord," although not in the aristocratic sense.**

-kun **is used by persons of superior rank to their juniors. It can sometimes have a familiar connotation.**

-san **is a standard honorific similar to Mr., Mrs., Miss or Ms.**

-sama **is used with people of much higher rank.**

Julietta Suzuki's debut manga *Hoshi ni Naru Hi* (The Day One Becomes a Star) appeared in the 2004 *Hana to Yume Plus*. Her other books include *Akuma to Dolce* (The Devil and Sweets) and *Karakuri Odette*. Born in December in Fukuoka Prefecture, she enjoys having movies play in the background while she works on her manga.

KAMISAMA KISS
VOL. 19
Shojo Beat Edition

STORY AND ART BY
Julietta Suzuki

English Translation & Adaptation/Tomo Kimura
Touch-up Art & Lettering/Joanna Estep
Design/Yukiko Whitley
Editor/Pancha Diaz

KAMISAMA HAJIMEMASHITA by Julietta Suzuki
© Julietta Suzuki 2014
All rights reserved.
First published in Japan in 2014 by HAKUSENSHA, Inc., Tokyo.
English language translation rights arranged with
HAKUSENSHA, Inc., Tokyo.

The stories, characters and incidents mentioned
in this publication are entirely fictional.

No portion of this book may be reproduced or transmitted
in any form or by any means without written permission
from the copyright holders.

Printed in the U.S.A.

Published by VIZ Media, LLC
P.O. Box 77010
San Francisco, CA 94107

10 9 8 7 6 5 4 3 2 1
First printing, October 2015

www.viz.com

www.shojobeat.com

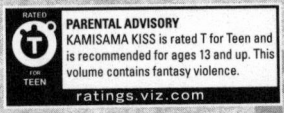

Natsume's BOOK of FRIENDS

STORY and ART by
Yuki Midorikawa

Make Some Unusual New Friends

The power to see hidden spirits has always felt like a curse to troubled high schooler Takashi Natsume. But he's about to discover he inherited a lot more than just the Sight from his mysterious grandmother!

Available at your local bookstore or comic store.

Shojo Beat
www.shojobeat.com

Natsume Yujincho © Yuki Midorikawa 2005/HAKUSENSHA, Inc.

RATED T FOR TEEN
ratings.viz.com

viz media
www.viz.co

This is the last page.

In keeping with the original Japanese comic format, this book reads from right to left—so action, sound effects, and word balloons are completely reversed. This preserves the orientation of the original artwork—plus, it's fun! Check out the diagram shown here to get the hang of things, and then turn to the other side of the book to get started!